Diabetic Baking Cookbook

Healthy Diabetic Friendly Baking Recipes You Can Easily Make!

Table of Contents

Introduction

Chapter 1: Diabetic Bread And Muffin Recipes

High Fiber Whole Wheat Bread

Banana Bread

Spiced Cream Cheese Banana Bread

Hazelnut Banana Loaf

Pumpkin Orange Loaf

Walnut Orange Mini Muffins

Pineapple Banana Bread

Carrot Raisin Muffins

Cherry Banana Mini Loafs

Lemon Orange Loaf

Pumpkin Orange Muffins

Cornbread

Cranberry Banana Bread

Cherry Banana Bread

Applesauce Muffins

Chapter 2: Diabetic Friendly Cake Recipes

Lime Cheesecake

Raspberry Coffee Cake

Chocolate Brownies

Cream Cheese Butterscotch Cake

Pineapple Cake

Strawberry Marble Cake

Peanut Butter Crumb Cake

Coffee Oatmeal Cake

White Chocolate Cake

Berry Coffee Cake

Orange Nut Cake

Lemon Cake

Introduction

The baking recipes in this cookbook have a focus on avoiding sugars, excessive amounts of fat, and calories which is important for anyone with diabetes. Since most baking recipes are loaded with sugar, fat and calories it can be very hard finding decent baking recipes for diabetics.

The recipes in this cookbook are my favorite diabetic friendly recipes. We hope you enjoy these diabetic baking recipes, good luck!

Chapter 1: Diabetic Bread And Muffin Recipes

High Fiber Whole Wheat Bread

Ingredients

2 cups white whole wheat flour

½ cup ground flaxseeds or flaxseed meal

2 teaspoons baking powder

½ teaspoon baking soda

¼ teaspoon salt

1 egg, lightly beaten

1½ cups buttermilk

¼ cup vegetable oil

2 tablespoons Splenda

cooking spray

Directions

Preheat oven to 350°F. Lightly coat a 9x5-inch loaf pan with cooking spray.

In a large bowl stir together the flour, flaxseeds, baking powder, baking soda and salt. Make a well in center of flour mixture.

In a medium bowl combine the egg, buttermilk, oil and sugar. Add all at once to flour mixture. Stir just until moistened. Spread batter in the prepared pan.

Bake 45 to 50 minutes or until a toothpick comes out clean. Cool in pan 10 minutes. Remove bread from pan; cool on a wire rack. If desired, wrap and store overnight before slicing.

Nutrition: 120 Calories; 5g Fat; 4g Protein; 15g Carbohydrates per 1/16 of recipe

Banana Bread

Ingredients

1½ cups all-purpose flour

1 teaspoon baking soda

1 teaspoon ground cinnamon

¼ teaspoon salt

⅛ teaspoon ground cloves

1 cup shredded sweet potato

⅔ cup mashed ripe bananas

1 (6 ounce) container plain fat-free Greek yogurt

½ cup packed brown sugar

½ cup refrigerated or frozen egg product, thawed

⅓ cup canola oil

¼ cup chopped pecans, toasted

Nonstick cooking spray

Directions

Preheat oven to 350°F. Coat bottom and sides of a 9x5x3-inch loaf pan with cooking spray; set aside. In a large bowl combine flour, baking soda, cinnamon, salt, and cloves. Make a well in the center of the flour mixture; set aside.

In a medium bowl stir together sweet potato, bananas, yogurt, brown sugar, eggs, and oil. Add egg mixture all at once to flour mixture; stir until evenly moistened. Fold in pecans. Spoon batter into prepared pan.

Bake 50 to 55 minutes or until a wooden toothpick inserted near the center comes out clean. If necessary to prevent overbrowning, cover loosely with foil for the last 15 minutes of baking. Cool in pan on a wire rack 10 minutes.

Remove from pan; cool completely on wire rack. Wrap in plastic wrap or foil; store overnight before slicing.

Nutrition: 143 Calories; 5g Fat; 3g Protein; 20g Carbohydrates per 1/16 of recipe

Spiced Cream Cheese Banana Bread

Ingredients

1½ cups all-purpose flour

¼ cup regular rolled oats

1½ teaspoons baking powder

¾ teaspoon ground cardamom

¾ teaspoon ground cinnamon

½ teaspoon baking soda

¼ teaspoon salt

¼ teaspoon ground cloves

¼ teaspoon ground allspice

4 egg whites

⅔ cup mashed ripe bananas (about 2 medium)

⅓ cup canola oil

¼ cup honey

¼ cup fat-free milk

4 ounces reduced-fat cream cheese, softened

2 tablespoons all-purpose flour

1 tablespoon honey

1 teaspoon vanilla

Directions

Preheat oven to 350°F. Lightly coat a 9x5x3-inch loaf pan with cooking spray. Line bottom of pan with parchment paper, if desired. Set aside. In a large bowl stir together the 1½ cups flour, the oats, baking powder, cardamom, cinnamon, baking soda, salt, cloves, and allspice. Make a well in the center of the flour mixture; set aside.

In a medium bowl combine 2 of the egg whites, the bananas, oil, the ¼ cup honey, and the milk.

In another medium bowl combine cream cheese, the remaining 2 egg whites, the 2 tablespoons flour, the 1 tablespoon honey, and the vanilla. Beat with an electric mixer on medium speed just until combined; set aside.

Add banana mixture all at once to flour mixture; stir until evenly moistened. Spoon two-thirds of the batter into the prepared baking pan. Spoon cream cheese mixture over batter in baking pan; spoon the remaining batter over all. Using a thin metal spatula or a table knife, cut down through the batter and pull up in a circular motion to marble the cream cheese layer.

Bake 50 to 60 minutes or until a wooden toothpick inserted near the center comes out clean. If necessary to prevent overbrowning, cover loosely with foil for the last 15 minutes of baking.

Cool in pan on a wire rack 10 minutes. Remove from pan; cool completely on wire rack. Wrap in plastic wrap or foil; chill in the refrigerator overnight before slicing.

Nutrition: 142 Calories; 7g Fat; 3g Protein; 18g Carbohydrates per 1/16 of recipe

Hazelnut Banana Loaf

Ingredients

1¾ cups all-purpose flour

2 tablespoons unsweetened cocoa powder

1 teaspoon baking soda

¼ teaspoon salt

2 eggs, lightly beaten

1 cup mashed ripe bananas

1 (6 ounce) container fat-free Greek yogurt, plain

½ cup packed Splenda brown sugar substitute

¼ cup chocolate-hazelnut spread

2 tablespoons canola oil

¼ cup chopped hazelnuts

Directions

Preheat oven to 350°F. Coat one 9x5x3-inch loaf pan or two 7x3½x2-inch loaf pans with cooking spray; if desired, line bottom with parchment paper. Set aside. In a large bowl combine flour, cocoa powder, baking soda, and salt. Make a well in the center of the flour mixture; set aside.

In a medium bowl combine eggs, bananas, yogurt, brown sugar, chocolate-hazelnut spread, and oil. Add banana mixture all at once to flour mixture; stir until evenly moistened. Spoon batter into prepared pan. Sprinkle top evenly with hazelnuts.

Bake 45 to 50 minutes for the 9x5x3-inch pan or 30 to 35 minutes for the 7x3½x2-inch pans or until a wooden toothpick inserted near the center comes out clean. If necessary to prevent overbrowning, cover loosely with foil for the last 15 minutes of baking.

Cool in pan on wire rack10 minutes. Remove from pan; cool completely on wire rack. Peel off parchment paper, if using. Wrap in plastic wrap or foil; store overnight before slicing.

Nutrition: 152 Calories; 5g Fat; 4g Protein; 23g Carbohydrates per 1/16 of recipe

Pumpkin Orange Loaf

Ingredients

2 cups all-purpose flour

1⅓ cups whole wheat flour

2 teaspoons baking powder

1 teaspoon ground nutmeg

½ teaspoon salt

½ teaspoon baking soda

1 (15 ounce) can pumpkin

¾ cup Splenda

1 cup refrigerated or frozen egg product, thawed, or 4 eggs, slightly beaten

½ cup honey

⅓ cup cooking oil

1 teaspoon finely shredded orange peel

⅓ cup orange juice

½ cup chopped walnuts or pecans

½ cup snipped pitted dates or raisins

Directions

Preheat oven to 350°F. Grease the bottom and ½ inch up the sides of two 8x2-inch loaf pans or line bottoms with parchment paper; set aside. In a large bowl, stir together all-purpose flour, whole wheat flour, baking powder, nutmeg, salt, and baking soda. Set aside.

In a medium bowl, stir together pumpkin, Splenda, egg, honey, oil, orange peel, and orange juice.

Using a wooden spoon, stir pumpkin mixture into flour mixture just until combined. Stir in nuts and dates or raisins. Divide mixture between the prepared pans.

Bake about 50 minutes or until a toothpick inserted near centers comes out clean. Cool in pans on wire racks for 10 minutes. Remove from pans. Cool completely on wire racks.

Nutrition: 130 calories; 4g fat; 23 g carbohydrates; 3g protein; per 1/32 of recipe

Walnut Orange Mini Muffins

Ingredients

1 cup Splenda

1/4 cup (1/2 stick) light butter

1 egg

2 teaspoons grated orange peel

1/2 teaspoon vanilla extract

1/8 teaspoon ground cinnamon

2 cups whole wheat flour

1 teaspoon baking soda

1/2 cup freshly squeezed orange juice

1/2 cup water

1/2 cup chopped walnuts

Directions

Preheat the oven to 350 degrees. Coat mini muffin pans with cooking spray.

In a medium bowl, cream the Splenda and butter. Add the egg, orange peel, vanilla extract, and cinnamon; mix well.

14

In another medium bowl, combine the flour and baking soda. Add the flour mixture, orange juice, and water to the sugar mixture; stir until well combined. Stir in the walnuts then distribute the mixture evenly into the mini muffin cups.

Bake for 15 to 18 minutes, or until a wooden toothpick inserted in the center comes out clean. Serve warm.

Nutrition: 77 calories; 2g fat; 13g carbohydrates; 2g protein; per muffin

Pineapple Banana Bread

Ingredients

1 cup all-purpose flour

1 cup whole-wheat flour

¼ cup flaked coconut, toasted

1 teaspoon baking soda

1 teaspoon ground ginger

¼ teaspoon salt

⅔ cup mashed ripe bananas

1 (6 ounce) container plain nonfat Greek yogurt

½ cup liquid egg substitute

⅓ cup packed Splenda brown sugar substitute

¼ cup canned crushed pineapple (juice pack), well drained

¼ cup margarine, melted

1 teaspoon vanilla

Directions

Preheat oven to 350°F. Coat bottom and sides of a 9x5x3-inch loaf pan with cooking spray or line with parchment paper; set aside. In a large bowl combine flours, coconut, baking soda, ginger, and salt. Make a well in the center of the flour mixture; set aside.

In a medium bowl combine bananas, yogurt, eggs, Splenda, pineapple, melted margarine, and vanilla. Add egg mixture all at once to the flour mixture; stir until evenly moistened. Spoon batter into prepared pan.

Bake 55 to 60 minutes or until a wooden toothpick inserted near the center comes out clean. If necessary to prevent overbrowning, cover loosely with foil for the last 15 minutes of baking. Cool in pan on a wire rack 10 minutes.

Remove from pan; cool completely on wire rack. Wrap in plastic wrap or foil; store overnight before slicing.

Nutrition: 120 calories; 4g fat; 19 g carbohydrates; 4 g protein per 1/16 of recipe

Carrot Raisin Muffins

Ingredients

1 1/2 cups all-purpose flour

1/2 cup whole-wheat flour

3/4 cup Splenda

1 tablespoon ground cinnamon

1 teaspoon baking powder

1 teaspoon baking soda

1/2 teaspoon salt

1 1/2 cups grated carrots (4 medium)

1/2 cup raisins

1 large egg

2 large egg whites

3/4 cup fruit purée fat replacement or apple butter

2 tablespoons vegetable oil

1 tablespoon vanilla extract

2 tablespoons finely chopped pecans or walnuts

Directions

Lightly spray 12 muffin cups or line with paper-liners; set aside.

Whisk flours, Splenda, cinnamon, baking powder, baking soda and salt in large bowl. Stir in carrots and raisins.

Whisk egg, egg whites, fruit purée, oil and vanilla in small bowl. Stir into dry ingredients until just moistened.

Spoon batter into muffin cups; sprinkle with nuts, if desired. Bake in preheated 375°F oven 18 to 20 minutes or until tops spring back when lightly pressed. Cool in pan 10 minutes.

Remove muffins from pan and cool on wire rack. Serve warm or at room temperature.

Nutrition: 180 calories; 3g fat; 35g carbohydrates; 4g protein; per muffin

Cherry Banana Mini Loafs

Makes 8 small loafs

Ingredients

¾ cup whole-wheat flour

1 cup all-purpose flour

½ cup regular rolled oats

1 teaspoon baking soda

1 teaspoon ground cinnamon

¼ teaspoon kosher salt

¼ cup margarine, softened

½ cup Splenda

1 (6 ounce) container plain nonfat Greek yogurt

¾ cup liquid egg substitute

⅔ cup mashed ripe bananas

¼ cup fat-free milk

1 teaspoon vanilla

1½ cups cherry berry blend frozen fruit

Directions

Preheat oven to 350°F. Lightly coat 8 mini loaf pans with cooking spray. Line bottoms of pans with parchment paper or wax paper; set aside. In a large bowl, combine flours, oats, baking soda, cinnamon, and kosher salt.

In a medium bowl, beat margarine with an electric mixer on medium to high speed 30 seconds. Gradually add Splenda, beating until combined; scrape sides of bowl and beat 2 minutes more. Beat in yogurt, egg, banana, milk, and vanilla.

Add the banana mixture to the flour mixture all at once; stir until moistened. Cut large pieces of frozen fruit into small pieces. Set aside about ¼ cup of the fruit. Fold the remaining fruit into the batter. Divide batter among prepared loaf pans. Sprinkle the reserved fruit on the tops of the loaves.

Bake 30 to 35 minutes or until a wooden toothpick inserted near centers comes out clean. Cool in pans on a wire rack 5 minutes. Remove from pans and cool completely on wire racks.

Nutrition: 135 calories; 3g fat; 22 g carbohydrates; 4 g protein; per 1/16 of recipe

Lemon Orange Loaf

Ingredients

2 cups all-purpose flour

1 teaspoon baking powder

1/2 teaspoon baking soda

2/3 cup 1% milk

2 tablespoons lemon juice

1 1/2 teaspoons freshly grated lemon peel

1 1/2 teaspoons freshly grated orange peel

2 large eggs

3/4 cup Splenda

1/2 cup margarine, melted

2 teaspoons vanilla extract

3/4 cup chopped walnuts

Directions

Preheat oven to 350°F (175°F). Lightly spray an 8x4-inch loaf pan with vegetable cooking spray.

Combine flour, baking powder, and baking soda. Set aside. Combine milk, lemon juice, lemon and orange peel. Set aside.

Beat eggs and Splenda on high speed with an electric mixer for 5 minutes. Reduce speed to medium; gradually add melted butter and vanilla, beating until blended, about 1 minute.

Add flour mixture alternately with milk mixture; beginning and ending with flour mixture. Beat at low speed until blended after each addition. Stir in nuts. Spoon batter into prepared loaf pan.

Bake 30 to 35 minutes or until a long wooden pick inserted in center comes out clean. Cool in pan on a wire rack 10 minutes; remove from pan and cool completely.

Nutrition: 220 calories; 14g fat; 20g carbohydrates; 5g protein

Pumpkin Orange Muffins

Ingredients

1⅓ cups all-purpose flour

¾ cup buckwheat flour

¼ cup sugar plus 2 packages heat-stable sugar substitute

1½ teaspoons baking powder

1 teaspoon ground cinnamon

½ teaspoon baking soda

½ teaspoon salt

2 eggs, lightly beaten

1 cup canned pumpkin

½ cup fat-free milk

2 tablespoons cooking oil

½ teaspoon finely shredded orange peel

¼ cup orange juice

Directions

Spray twelve 2- ½-inch muffin cups with nonstick coating; set pan aside. In a medium bowl combine the all-purpose flour, buckwheat flour, sugar plus sugar substitute or the sugar, baking powder, cinnamon, baking soda, and salt. Make a well in the center of flour mixture; set aside.

In another bowl combine the eggs, pumpkin, milk, oil, orange. peel, and orange juice. Add the egg mixture all at once to the four mixture. Stir just until moistened, batter will be lumpy.

Spoon batter into the prepared muffin cups, dividing the batter evenly. Bake in a 400°F oven for 15 to 20 minutes or until the muffins are light brown. Cool in muffin cups on wire rack for 5 minutes. Remove from muffin cups; serve warm.

Nutrition: 134 calories; 4g fat; 22g carbohydrates; 4g protein per muffin

Cornbread

Ingredients

1¼ cups yellow cornmeal, preferably whole-grain

¾ cup white whole-wheat flour

1 teaspoon baking powder

½ teaspoon salt

1 cup corn kernels, fresh or frozen, thawed

1 large egg

¾ cup low-fat milk

3 tablespoons canola oil

3 tablespoons Truvia

Directions

Preheat oven to 350°F. Coat an 8-inch-square baking pan with cooking spray.

Whisk cornmeal, flour, baking powder and salt in a large bowl. Pulse corn and egg in a food processor or blender until almost smooth. Add milk, oil and Truvia; pulse until combined.

Add the liquid ingredients to the dry ingredients and stir until just combined. Scrape the batter into the prepared pan, spreading evenly.

Bake the cornbread until a toothpick inserted in the center comes out clean, 25 to 30 minutes. Let cool in the pan for at least 10 minutes. Serve warm or at room temperature.

Nutrition: 188 calories; 6g fat; 30g carbohydrates; 5g protein per 1/9 of recipe

Cranberry Banana Bread

Ingredients

1½ cups all-purpose flour

½ cup whole wheat flour

½ cup dried cranberries

⅓ cup sliced almonds

1½ teaspoons baking powder

1 teaspoon ground cinnamon

½ teaspoon baking soda

¼ teaspoon salt

⅔ cup mashed ripe bananas

½ cup liquid egg substitute

⅓ cup honey

⅓ cup orange juice

¼ cup butter, melted

¼ teaspoon almond extract

Nonstick cooking spray

Directions

Preheat oven to 350°F. Coat the bottom and sides of a 9x5x3-inch loaf pan with cooking spray or line with parchment paper. In a large bowl combine flours, cranberries, almonds, baking powder, cinnamon, baking soda, and salt. Make a well in the center of the flour mixture; set aside.

In a medium bowl combine bananas, eggs, honey, orange juice, melted butter, and almond extract. Add egg mixture all at once to flour mixture; stir until evenly moistened. Spoon batter into prepared pan.

Bake about 45 minutes or until a wooden toothpick inserted near the center comes out clean. If necessary to prevent overbrowning, cover loosely with foil for the last 15 minutes of baking.

Cool in pan on a wire rack 10 minutes. Remove from pan; cool completely on wire rack. Wrap in plastic wrap or foil; store overnight before slicing.

Nutrition: 38 calories; 4g fat; 23 g carbohydrates; 3 g protein; per 1/16 of recipe

Cherry Banana Bread

Ingredients

1½ cups all-purpose flour

⅔ cup Splenda

2 teaspoons baking powder

¼ teaspoon baking soda

¼ cup fat-free dairy sour cream

¼ cup skim milk

1 egg beaten

2 teaspoons cooking oil

⅔ cup mashed banana

1 teaspoon vanilla

8 maraschino cherries, drained and chopped

¼ cup chopped walnuts

Directions

Preheat oven to 350°F. Lightly coat the bottom and ½ inch up sides of a 9x5x3-inch loaf pan with nonstick cooking spray. Line bottom of pan with parchment paper and coat with cooking spray, if desired. Set aside.

In a large bowl, stir together all-purpose flour, sugar, baking powder, and baking soda. Make a well in center of flour mixture; set aside.

In a medium bowl, combine sour cream, milk, egg, and oil. Stir in mashed banana and vanilla.

Add sour cream mixture all at once to flour mixture; stir just until moistened. Fold in chopped cherries, and walnuts.

Spoon batter into prepared pan. Bake for 35 to 40 minutes or until a toothpick inserted near the center comes out clean. Cool in pan on a wire rack for 10 minutes. Remove bread from pan. Cool completely on wire rack.

Nutrition: 173 calories; 7g fat; 26g carbohydrates; 2g protein per 1/16 of recipe

Applesauce Muffins

Ingredients

1½ cups whole-wheat flour

⅔ cup bran cereal

1 teaspoon baking soda

½ teaspoon ground cinnamon

½ teaspoon salt

½ cup chopped dates

¼ cup chopped walnuts, toasted

1 large egg, lightly beaten

1¾ cups unsweetened applesauce

⅓ cup packed Splenda brown sugar substitute

2 tablespoons canola oil

Directions

Preheat oven to 425°F. Coat 12 muffin cups with cooking spray.

Whisk flour, bran cereal, baking soda, cinnamon and salt in a large bowl. Stir in dates and walnuts. Whisk egg, applesauce, brown sugar and oil in another bowl until smooth.

Make a well in the dry ingredients; add the wet ingredients and stir with a rubber spatula until just combined, do not over mix. Spoon the batter into the prepared muffin cups.

Bake the muffins until the tops are golden brown and spring back when touched lightly, 12 to 15 minutes.

Let cool in the pan for 5 minutes. Loosen edges and turn muffins out onto a wire rack to cool.

Nutrition: 160 calories; 5g fat; 4g fiber; 29g carbohydrates; 4g protein; per muffin

Chapter 2: Diabetic Friendly Cake Recipes

Lime Cheesecake

Ingredients

Crust:

1 cup graham cracker crumbs

3 tablespoons margarine, melted

2 tablespoons Splenda

Cheesecake:

2 (8-ounce each) packages reduced-fat cream cheese, softened

2/3 cup Splenda

1 large egg

2 large egg whites

1/2 teaspoon grated lime peel

3 tablespoon fresh lime juice

Additional grated lime peel

Directions

To Make Crust: Combine graham cracker crumbs, butter and 2 tablespoons Splenda Press onto bottom and 1/2-inch up side of an 8-inch springform pan or 8-inch round cake pan. Bake in preheated 325°F oven for 8 minutes. Cool on wire rack while preparing cheesecake.

To Make Cheesecake: Beat cream cheese and 2/3 cup Splenda in mixing bowl on medium speed of mixer until smooth and well combined. Mix in egg, egg whites, lime peel and juice until well blended.

Pour cream cheese mixture over baked crust. Bake in preheated oven 30 to 35 minutes or until center of cake is almost set. Cool on wire rack.

Gently run metal spatula around rim of pan to loosen cake. Let cheesecake cool completely. Cover and refrigerate several hours or overnight before serving.

To serve, remove side of pan. Garnish top of cheesecake with grated lime peel, if desired. Cut cake into wedges.

Nutrition: 197 calories; 11g fat; 14g carbohydrates; 9g protein; per 1/8 of recipe

Raspberry Coffee Cake

Ingredients

3 tablespoons margarine, softened

3/4 cup Splenda, divided

1/4 cup plus 2 tablespoons egg substitute, divided

1 teaspoon grated lemon peel

1 teaspoon vanilla extract

1-1/4 cups all-purpose flour

1-1/4 teaspoons baking powder

1/4 teaspoon baking soda

1/4 teaspoon salt

1/2 cup buttermilk

1 cup fresh raspberries

2 ounces reduced-fat cream cheese

1 teaspoon confectioners' sugar

Directions

In a large mixing bowl, beat margarine and 1/2 cup Splenda until crumbly, about 2 minutes. Beat in 1/4 cup egg substitute, lemon peel and vanilla. Combine the flour, baking powder, baking soda and salt; add to butter mixture alternately with buttermilk.

Pour into a 9-in. springform pan coated with cooking spray; sprinkle with berries. In a small mixing bowl, beat cream cheese and remaining sugar until fluffy. Beat in remaining egg substitute. Pour over berries.

Place pan on a baking sheet. Bake at 375F° for 25-30 minutes or until a toothpick inserted near the center comes out clean. Cool on a wire rack for 10 minutes.

Carefully run a knife around edge of pan to loosen; remove sides of pan. Sprinkle with confectioners' sugar.

Nutrition: 221 calories; 6g fat; 37g carbohydrates; 5g protein; per 1/8 of recipe

Chocolate Brownies

Ingredients

6 tablespoons margarine, softened

1/2 cup unsweetened applesauce

2 large eggs

1 teaspoon vanilla extract

3/4 cup all-purpose flour

1 cup Splenda

1/2 cup semisweet chocolate chips

6 tablespoons unsweetened cocoa

1 teaspoon baking powder

1/4 teaspoon salt

Directions

Beat margarine, applesauce, eggs, and vanilla until blended. Stir in combined flour, margarine, chocolate chips, Splenda, cocoa, baking powder and salt until blended.

Spread batter in sprayed 8-inch square baking pan. Bake in a preheated 350F oven 18 to 20 minutes or until top springs back when gently touched. Cool completely on wire rack. Cut into squares.

Store in airtight container at room temperature.

Nutrition: 105 calories; 7g fat; 10g carbohydrates; 2g protein; per 1/16 of recipe

Cream Cheese Butterscotch Cake

Ingredients

1-1/2 cups graham cracker crumbs

Sugar substitute equivalent to 1/2 cup sugar, divided

6 tablespoons butter, melted

2 packages reduced-fat cream cheese

3 cups cold fat-free milk, divided

2 packages sugar-free instant butterscotch pudding mix

1 carton frozen reduced-fat whipped topping, thawed

1/2 teaspoon rum extract

Directions

In a small bowl, combine the cracker crumbs, 1/4 cup sugar substitute and butter. Press into a 13-in. x 9-in. dish coated with cooking spray.

In a small bowl, beat the cream cheese, 1/4 cup milk and remaining sugar substitute until smooth. Spread over crust.

In another bowl, whisk remaining milk with the pudding mix for 2 minutes. Let stand for 2 minutes or until soft-set. Gently spread over cream cheese layer.

Combine whipped topping and extract; spread over the top. Refrigerate for at least 4 hours.

Nutrition: 136 calories; 8g fat; 12g carbohydrates; 3g protein; per 1/24 of recipe

Pineapple Cake

Ingredients

3 bananas, mashed

1 cup yellow sugar free cake mix

1/3 cup whole wheat flour

1/4 cup crushed pineapple packed in juice, not drained

2/3 cup fat-free liquid egg substitute

1/2 cup Splenda Sugar Blend sweetener

1 teaspoon cinnamon

1 teaspoon baking powder

1 teaspoon vanilla extract

Frosting

3 ounces reduced-fat cream cheese

1 tablespoon Splenda Sugar Blend sweetener

1 tablespoon chopped pecans

Directions

Preheat oven to 350 degrees F. Coat a 9-inch round cake pan with cooking spray.

In a large bowl, combine bananas, cake mix, flour, pineapple with its juice, egg substitute, 1/2 cup Splenda, cinnamon, baking powder, and vanilla wth a wooden spoon until batter is well mixed. Pour into prepared cake pan.

Bake 30 to 35 minutes, or until a toothpick inserted in center comes out clean. Let cool 10 to 15 minutes, then invert onto wire rack to cool completely.

In a medium bowl, mix cream cheese and 1 tablespoon Splenda until smooth. Spread evenly on top of cake, sprinkle with pecans, and serve.

Nutrition: 195 calories; 4g fat; 24g carbohydrates; 4g protein; per 1/10 of recipe

Strawberry Marble Cake

Ingredients

1-1/2 cups egg whites (about 10)

1 package (10 ounces) frozen unsweetened strawberries, thawed and drained

1-1/2 cups Splenda, divided

1-1/4 cups cake flour

1-1/2 teaspoons cream of tartar

1/2 teaspoon salt

1 teaspoon vanilla extract

1 teaspoon almond extract

Red food coloring, optional

Directions

Let egg whites stand at room temperature for 30 minutes. In a food processor, puree strawberries; strain puree and discard seeds. Set aside.

Sift together 3/4 cup sugar and the flour twice; set aside. Add cream of tartar and salt to egg whites; beat on medium speed until soft peaks form. Gradually beat in remaining sugar, 2 tablespoons at a time, on high until stiff glossy peaks form and sugar is dissolved. Gradually fold in flour mixture, about 1/2 cup at a time.

Transfer half of the batter to another bowl; fold in extracts. Fold 1/4 cup strawberry puree into remaining batter; add food coloring if desired.

Gently spoon batters, alternating colors, into an ungreased 10-in. tube pan. Cut through with a knife to swirl. Bake at 350° for 45-50 minutes or until lightly browned and top appears dry. Immediately invert pan; cool completely, about 1 hour.

Nutrition: 176 calories; 0 fat; 39g carbohydrate; 5g protein; per 1/12 of recipe

Peanut Butter Crumb Cake

Ingredients

1 (6.5-ounce) package sugar-free chocolate sandwich cookies

2 tablespoons margarine, melted

1 (8-ounce) package reduced-fat cream cheese, softened

3/4 cup reduced-fat peanut butter

1 tablespoon sugar substitute

1 (8-ounce) container sugar-free frozen whipped topping, thawed

1 (1.4-ounce) package instant sugar-free, fat-free chocolate pudding

1 1/2 cup skim milk

Directions

Place cookies in a resealable plastic bag; using a rolling pin, crush cookies. Reserve 2 tablespoons, then place remaining cookies in a medium bowl. Add margarine and mix well. Press crumb mixture into bottom of a 9-inch springform pan. Chill until ready to use.

In a large bowl, beat cream cheese, peanut butter, and sugar substitute until creamy. Stir in whipped topping until completely mixed. Evenly spread over cookie crust.

In a large bowl, whisk pudding and milk until thickened. Spread over cream cheese layer.

Sprinkle with reserved cookie crumbs and garnish with gummy worms, if desired. Refrigerate 4 hours, or until ready to serve.

Nutrition: 207 calories; 13g fat; 18g carbohydrates; 6g protein; per 1/16 of recipe

Coffee Oatmeal Cake

Ingredients

1/3 cup canola oil

1/2 cup egg substitute

1/4 cup sugar substitute

1/2 cup plus 1 tablespoon brown sugar, divided

1 teaspoon vanilla extract

3/4 cup quick-cooking oatmeal, prepared in water

3/4 cup white whole wheat flour

3/4 cup all-purpose flour

1 teaspoon cinnamon

1/2 teaspoon salt

1 teaspoon baking soda

1/4 cup chopped walnuts

Directions

Preheat oven to 350 F. Coat an 8-inch square baking dish with cooking spray.

In a large bowl, combine oil, egg substitute, sugar substitute, 1/2 cup brown sugar, the vanilla, and oatmeal; mix well.

In a medium bowl, combine both flours, cinnamon, salt, and baking soda; mix well. Stir flour mixture into egg mixture until well combined. Pour into baking dish.

In a small bowl, mix walnuts and remaining brown sugar; sprinkle over batter.

Bake 30 to 35 minutes, or until toothpick inserted in center comes out dry. Let cool, then cut into squares.

Nutrition: 152 calories; 8g fat; 17g carbohydrates; 4g protein; per 1/12 of recipe

White Chocolate Cake

Ingredients

1 ounce white chocolate baking squares

1 tablespoon fat-free milk

1 1/2 stick light margarine

3/4 cup sugar substitute

4 eggs, separated

2 tablespoons lemon zest

1 teaspoon lemon extract

2 1/2 cups almond flour

2 tablespoons lemon juice

Directions

Preheat oven to 350 F. Line a 9-inch cake pan with wax paper.

In a small microwaveable bowl, combine white chocolate and milk. Microwave for 30 seconds, stir, and continue to microwave at 10-second intervals until smooth; set aside.

In a large bowl, beat margarine and 3/4 cup sugar substitute until fluffy. Add the egg yolks, lemon zest, and lemon extract; beat until combined. Add the almond flour, melted chocolate and lemon juice; beat until well combined.

In a medium bowl, beat egg whites and remaining tablespoon of sugar substitute until soft peaks form. Fold the egg whites into the batter until well combined. Spoon the batter into cake pan.

Bake 40-45 minutes, or until toothpick inserted in center comes out clean. Let cool 30 minutes, then invert onto a platter, remove wax paper, and turn cake over. Let cool completely.

Nutrition: 205 calories; 19g fat; 2g carbohydrates; 5.5g protein; per 1/16 of recipe

Berry Coffee Cake

Ingredients

1-3/4 cups all-purpose flour, divided

1-1/2 teaspoons baking powder

1/2 teaspoon salt

1/4 teaspoon baking soda

2 egg whites

1 egg

2/3 cup unsweetened applesauce

1/4 cup plain low fat yogurt

2 tablespoons sugar

1 teaspoon grated lemon peel

1 package frozen unsweetened mixed berries

1/4 cup packed Splenda brown sugar substitute

2 tablespoons cold butter

8 tablespoons reduced-fat whipped topping

Directions

In a small bowl, combine 1-1/2 cups flour, baking powder, salt and baking soda. In another bowl, whisk the egg whites, egg, applesauce, yogurt, sugar and lemon peel; add to flour mixture, stirring gently until blended.

Spread into a 9-in. round baking pan coated with cooking spray; sprinkle with berries. In a small bowl, combine brown sugar and remaining flour; cut in butter until mixture resembles fine crumbs. Sprinkle over berries.

Bake at 350° for 35-40 minutes or until a toothpick inserted near the center comes out clean. Cool on a wire rack for 15 minutes. Serve with whipped topping.

Nutrition: 218 calories; 4g fat; 39g carbohydrates; 5g protein; per 1/8 of recipe

Orange Nut Cake

Ingredients

1 egg

1/3 cup stick margarine

1/3 cup Splenda

1/4 cup Splenda brown sugar blend

1 1/4 cup whole wheat flour

2 teaspoons baking powder

1/4 teaspoon baking soda

1/4 teaspoon cinnamon

1/3 cup reduced-sugar and calorie orange juice

2 teaspoons orange extract

2 tablespoons nuts, chopped

Directions

Preheat oven to 350 F. Coat an 8-inch square baking dish with cooking spray.

In a large bowl with an electric mixer, combine egg, margarine, granulated Splenda, and Splenda brown sugar. Beat 2 minutes at high speed, scraping down the bowl occasionally. Add in flour and mix well. Add in remaining ingredients, except nuts and mix 1 minute on low speed. Pour into prepared baking dish. Sprinkle with nuts.

Bake 20 to 25 minutes or until a toothpick inserted into center comes out clean.

Nutrition: 138 calories; 9g fat; 13g carbohydrates; 3g protein; per 1/10 of recipe

Lemon Cake

Ingredients

1 package yellow cake mix

1 package sugar-free lemon gelatin

3/4 cup egg substitute

1 can apricot nectar

1/2 cup unsweetened applesauce

2 tablespoons canola oil

1 teaspoon lemon extract

Directions

In a large mixing bowl, combine the first seven ingredients. Beat on medium speed for 2 minutes. Coat a 10-in. fluted tube pan with cooking spray and dust with flour; add the batter.

Bake at 350F° for 35-40 minutes or until a toothpick inserted near the center comes out clean. Cool for 10 minutes before removing to a wire rack.

Nutrition: 227 calories, 5g fat, 41g carbohydrate , 3g protein; per 1/14 of recipe

Printed in Great Britain
by Amazon

65333643R00038